RITUAL
ASSESSMENT

Ritual, Assessment
Copyright © 2021 by Man in the Mirror, Inc.

All rights reserved. No part of this publication may be reproduced in any form without prior permission of the publisher.

ISBN 979-8-9867859-0-5

Content contributors: Jeremy Schurke, John Seel, Louis Schieferdecker, and Parker Johnson
Cover design: Jeremy Kennedy
Layout and interior design: Jeremy Kennedy

Published by Man in the Mirror Press
1375 State Road 436
Casselberry, FL 32707
(407) 472-2100

Man in the Mirror Press is an imprint of Man in the Mirror, Inc.

Printed in the USA

CONTENTS

INTRODUCTION — V
HOW TO USE THIS JOURNAL — VII

HEALTH — 01
DIET
MOVEMENT
REST

ORIGINS — 17
HISTORY
PARENTS
WOUNDS

TRIBE — 35
FRIENDSHIP
MARRIAGE
PARENTING

VOCATION — 51
PURPOSE
CAREER
STEWARDSHIP

SOUL — 67
LOCATION
DIRECTION
COMMUNITY

NEXT STEPS — 83

INTRODUCTION

For many men, profound friendships with other men are exceptionally challenging to find and develop.

Much of our culture today is hyper-focused on romantic relationships, as well as mass communications. Through technology, we are overly connected yet wholly detached, with many of our connections floating along the surface level.

As a result, we are more isolated, lonely, and depressed than previous generations of men. We experience each other from a distance, in the shallows of life, often missing the depth and intimacy that comes from meaningful human interaction. If we are honest with ourselves, we long to be recognized, understood, and cared for on a soul level.

Meanwhile, the seeds of post-modernism have blossomed and pushed our culture into meaningless chaos. Truth has become relative and our values arbitrary. I believe every human longs to discover some sacred order that provides a foundation to build their life upon. And here lies the rub. Humans are created with a desire for meaning, so without common purpose the world goes mad.

So, in order to avoid being swept away in the aimless currents of our times, I sought out some concrete ways to provide sacred order to my life. To do this, I began to implement the constructive rituals of self-reflection and regular, meaningful conversations with other men. These two rituals have helped me focus on what's important as well as provided me some much-needed clarity.

This is why I wrote this journal.

Personally, I have come to the realization that to live more fully, to love deeply, and to keep my sanity, I need close, spiritual friendships—relationships where my secret thoughts, greatest desires, and ugliest parts are all welcome.

To have a soul-level friendship of this kind is to awaken belonging, foster deep healing, and grow true affection. I recognize this might sound awkward to some of you. And to others, it would be an answered prayer.

The collective wisdom of human history affirms the importance of exploring the depths of your life through self-reflection *and* sharing your observations with others.

This assessment serves as a diagnostic tool to help you do both. Men are particularly good at hiding our innermost lives, thoughts, and feelings—not just from each other but also from ourselves. Yet an honest life assessment is the first and most crucial step in becoming the man you were made to be.

My hope is that upon completion of *Ritual: Assessment*, you will have unearthed some of your own deficiencies, set new goals to pursue a life more in line with your desires and values, and developed authentic friendships along the way.

Aristotle stated, *"Nobody would choose to live without friends even if he had all other good things."*

Profound friendship for men *is* possible—friendships in which you are recognized by those who want your good and deeply care for you, and where you can wrestle through hard things together for your mutual benefit and growth.

Take the risk of inviting someone to go deeper with you.

Your friends will thank you later.

—Jeremy Schurke
Author

HOW TO USE THIS JOURNAL

The goal of *Ritual: Assessment* is twofold:

- Review your life to determine how to build a better one.
- Grow a deeper friendship with another man.

To succeed, there are four things you will need: the journal you are holding, a pen, at least one male friend who is willing to try this out with you, and the courage to vulnerably self-reflect and engage. That's it.

The process has two rotating cycles:

1) Sincerely reflect on your current life by journaling through prompts separated into five life categories: health, origins, tribe, vocation, and soul.

2) After completing each section's self-reflection portion on your own, it's time to discuss your observations with a trusted man in person. It's critical that you don't skip this part of the process.

To live a truly examined life will never be a solo endeavor.

Before you begin, you will need to pick someone who is willing to meet for in-person reviews. For the most impact, we recommend groups no larger than four (although two is preferred).

HOW TO BEGIN

To start, you need to pick a counterpart.

So, what do you look for when choosing someone?

Invite a man who is mutually committed to pursuing friendship through honesty.

You want someone who is "in" as much as you're willing to be "in." Let's not settle for another shallow acquaintanceship, born out of convenience.

Instead, try to pick someone who—like you—is interested in cultivating a deeper experience of friendship and self-examination. Have a conversation first about what you hope to get out of this assessment and then gauge his interest and commitment level.

Talk is cheap; actions define a man. Overall, this assessment will be greatly aided by the integrity of both participant's initial intentions and the degree of your collective self-reflection.

OVERVIEW

The sections of this journal correspond with the five major areas of a man's life: health, origins, tribe, vocation, and soul.

Each of these sections deserve at *least* an annual evaluation. We affirm that:

- Our bodies, as intrinsic parts of us, deserve attentive care and proper use.
- Our developmental experiences from an early age have shaped much of our personal values and views of the world, and have also left wounds.
- We have core relational needs to examine, prioritize, and pursue.
- We have the responsibility to choose how we dedicate our time and life's work.
- The core components that shape our lives are all established through our foundational beliefs about God and our transcendent views of reality.

To live a more meaningful life, a man must regularly measure these standards for living.

THE FLOW

All five sections have journaling sessions to be completed before a partner meet up. Each session includes quotes, short reflections, and writing prompts.

> **Quote and Reflection:** A brief introduction is provided to help **center yourself.** The goal is to pause, clear your mind of distractions, and become more present with the day's theme.
>
> **Writing Prompts:** There are daily questions to help you **explore your thoughts and experiences.** The goal is to think deeply on a particular topic and capture these thoughts in writing. Physically writing out your answers helps the mind slow down and process. **The prompts act as a guide for self-reflection; they are not an assignment to be completed.**

Each week ends with space to **rest and remember (R/R)**. Take some time to go back and reread your answers.

What do you see as your biggest challenges?

Are there specific goals you'd like to pursue?

Challenge yourself as you discover areas in need of improvement to share with each other.

There is also a subsequent page to write down your partner's biggest challenges and specific goals as well. For goals to be meaningful, they need to be written down, measured over time, and held up for mutual accountability.

The last step of this process is recording both of your **final conclusions**. These will give you valuable insights and concrete steps for moving forward after completing this journal!

A FINAL NOTE

The soul is a fragile and valuable thing, so remember to extend patience, grace, and gentleness as you go through this process—not just to your counterpart but to yourself.

Conduct your own investigation into your life and soul with curiosity and humility, that you might gain wisdom and grant some understanding to your friend in the process.

Let love for one another reign, that you both might benefit and grow—over the next few months and beyond.

Our hope is that *Ritual: Assessment* is the start of sacred practices in your life that promote clarity, order, and flourishment—and that it plays a small part in generating a revival of authentic male friendships in the years to come.

RITUAL

 HEALTH

ASSESSMENT

We are embodied beings. It all connects: the body, the mind, and the soul.

Neglecting our body's health will hinder every other aspect of our lives. Since our outward appearance and our internal attitudes are connected, let's start with what is physical and move our way inward. If we pay attention, our bodies continually reveal clues to us.

As an overall lifestyle, health involves three major aspects of embodiment: diet, movement, and rest.

For most men, health is a personal choice. To be successful though, our choices need to be reinforced through relationships.

DIET

FOOD

*"When diet is wrong, medicine is of no use.
When diet is correct, medicine is of no need."*
—AYURVEDIC PROVERB

Factory farming, processed foods, and many of the conveniences of modern life consistently work against maintaining a healthy lifestyle. To flourish in this area, as well as in the other parts of our lives, we must be resolute in our choices and resist the norms of society.

Is eating healthy a priority to you? Why or why not?

What foods do you most commonly eat?

Which unhealthy foods do you consume most often?

What steps do you take to regulate your eating habits?

Have you considered fasting regularly? Why or why not?

DRINK

"As an alcoholic, you will violate your standards quicker than you can lower them."
—ROBIN WILLIAMS

What we choose to drink impacts two important aspects of health: maintaining an ideal weight and revealing deeper identity issues. Sugary beverage intake increases the likelihood of obesity, heart failure and emotional imbalance. Careful attention must also be paid to excessive consumption of beverages acting as stimulants or depressants. Both coffee and alcohol can deceive our bodies about the physical and emotional realities lurking within.

Which drinks do you consume most often?

Other than water, do you regulate the amount you drink? If yes, which drinks and why?

If you had to cut back on one beverage, which would it be and why?

Do you drink alcohol? Why or why not?

On average, how much water do you drink daily?

MOVEMENT

SPORTS

"Nothing will work unless you do."
—JOHN WOODEN

We should continually evaluate and set forth fitness goals that align with the changing nature of a maturing life – work, marriage, family, and the like. We can't stay twenty and single forever! Many of the high school and college sports we once participated in become increasingly difficult to play as we grow older. We need to develop interests and skills in activities that we can incorporate across our entire life.

What has been your relationship with sports?

How has this changed as you have gotten older?

Do you have any outdoor hobbies?

Which activities would you like to participate in and grow your skills moving forward?

Is there an activity you've always wanted to try out? What's held you back?

EXERCISE

"If you think lifting is dangerous, try being weak. Being weak is dangerous."
—BRET CONTRERAS

Exercise needs to be framed by our desired outcomes. Daily discipline and routine fundamentally shape our preferred results. Bodies are designed to move. The less we engage them, the more they deteriorate. There are infinite ways to engage our bodies, and everyone is inclined to their particular preferences:

- cardiovascular vs. strength training
- team sports vs. individual sports
- flexibility vs. muscle mass
- primal vs. technical
- free flowing vs. regimented

What is the minimum amount of daily movement your body requires?

What would be your ideal amount of movement?

What type of movement do you enjoy most?

Do you have any fitness goals?

What is your greatest obstacle to achieving your goals?

Are you self-conscious about your body? Why or why not?

REST

PHYSICAL

*"Take rest;
a field that has rested
gives a bountiful crop"*
—OVID

Rest is a necessary function of optimal health.

This involves two things: regular sleep and scheduling regular time of reflection and meditation.

Due to the sheer number of evolving complexities awaiting us in this life, no man is able to sustain a healthy balance without incorporating routine rest into their schedule.

Ideally, rest involves a constructive routine of nightly sleep, a weekly Sabbath, and annual sabbaticals.

SLEEP

*"Sleep loss will leak down into every nook and cranny of your physiology. Sleep, unfortunately, is not an optional lifestyle luxury. Sleep is a nonnegotiable biological necessity.
It is your life support system."*
—MATTHEW WALKER, NEUROSCIENTIST

Many Americans sleep too little. Our bodies need sleep in order to function at their best. Rest demands discipline and a routine in order for us to achieve optimal health benefits.

Do you have a regular sleep schedule?

Do you get enough sleep? Why or why not?

How many hours does your body need to wake up well rested?

SABBATH

"There is virtue in work and there is virtue in rest. Use both and overlook neither."
—ALAN COHEN

Today's world is a 24/7/365 experience where technology has blended our home and work lives together. Our bodies are not designed for such a world. A sabbath is a weekly routine of consciously slowing down and devoting time for deep reflection.

Do you take a day off every week?

Is it valuable to you to set aside time to rest and remember? Why or why not?

What does a typical sabbath rest look like for you?

SABBATICAL

"As important as it is to have a plan for doing work, it is perhaps more important to have a plan for rest, relaxation, self-care, and sleep."
—AKIROQ BROST

A Sabbatical is multiple Sabbath days in unison. It is a prolonged rest in silence and solitude. A time to slow down, pay attention and rest your body and soul.

IF YOU WERE TO TAKE A 3 DAY SOLO RETREAT:

Where would you go?

What would you do?

REFLECTION

Of these three aspects of rest (nightly sleep, weekly rest, annual sabbatical), which happens most naturally and which is most difficult? Why?

What will it take to establish a routine in each of these areas of rest?

What are the benefits to your family, roommates, or close community if you maintained such routines?

How can they support or hinder your efforts?

MENTAL

"Your brain has more than 100 billion cells, each connected to at least 20,000 other cells. The possible combinations are greater than the number of molecules in the known universe."
—BRIAN TRACY

There are two mental aspects that require constant attention: stress and knowledge. To be human, we must contend with the daily stressors of life while evolving in our understanding of ourselves and the world around us. A rhythm between calming and stimulating is needed to fully develop our brains. We need daily routines of **stress reduction** and **active learning**.

STRESS

What causes you stress?

When are you least stressed? Most?

How do you deal with stress? What do you do to de-stress?

Who do you avoid when stressed and why?

LEARN

Under what conditions are you best able to learn?

What are your current barriers toward learning more?

What would you like to learn more about?

Is there anyone in your life that would be able to teach you about this?

REFLECTION

Which is most difficult for you: stress reduction or active learning?

What steps can you undertake to establish a better balance?

REST & REMEMBER: PERSONAL

REFLECT OVER THE PAST 6 DAYS

"Sabbath observance invites us to stop. It invites us to rest. It asks us to notice that while we rest, the world continues without our help. It invites us to delight in the world's beauty and abundance."
—WENDELL BERRY

BIGGEST HEALTH CHALLENGES:	SPECIFIC HEALTH GOALS:
Diet:	Diet:
Movement:	Movement:
Rest:	Rest:

NOTES:

REST & REMEMBER: PARTNER RECAP

NOTES:

BIGGEST HEALTH CHALLENGES:	SPECIFIC HEALTH GOALS:
Diet:	Diet:
Movement:	Movement:
Rest:	Rest:

RITUAL

HEALTH

ASSESSMENT

RITUAL

 ORIGINS

ASSESSMENT

Every person is a "we" before they are a "me." We were all born into specific families with unique histories that proceed us. Our families are *enormously* influential in our lives. They can establish our sense of self and form our understanding of the world. They can nurture, protect, and love us into mature, responsible adults. They can also damage us and be the greatest source of our wounds.

Family wounds are some of the most difficult to overcome and are prone to damage our other relationships. The failure to adequately examine our heritage, understand our family dynamics, and acknowledge the pain points of our childhood ultimately stunts our growth as humans. Every person needs to routinely explore their origins to develop a better sense of their current reality and determine how best to heal.

HISTORY

LINEAGE

"A people without the knowledge of their past history, origin and culture is like a tree without roots."
—MARCUS GARVEY

Beginning to understand our cultural background and origin story can help us develop a strong sense of identity. We are all born into a family, and that family is a combination of the culture, history, and traditions we inherited. Our family history provides us with a sense of belonging and creates a core identity that can be a great source of empowerment.

What do you know about your heritage?

Who were your great Grandparents?

What does your last name mean?

First name?

Do you have any family heirlooms?
If yes, what are they and do you find them important?

Do you communicate with your extended family? Why or why not?

CHILDHOOD

"Sometimes you have to grow up before you appreciate how you grew up."
—DANIEL BLACK

The first question ever conceived in childhood is also one of the most defining questions of personhood: *"What do I have to do to be loved?"*

Which leads to the natural follow up question: *"What must I do to make a difference?"*

Psychologically and spiritually, childhood is a pivotal time to learn self-acceptance and the resulting service to others.

Did you feel loved growing up?

Where did you find meaning and purpose in childhood?

What did you do for fun in elementary school?

Middle school?

High school?

Describe one of the happiest days of your childhood.

Describe one of the worst days of your childhood.

PARENTS

*"Children begin by loving their parents;
as they grow older they judge them;
sometimes they forgive them."*
—OSCAR WILDE

During the course of our lives, we experience a wide range of emotions towards our parents.

To honor them, we must consider our whole experience of them. Here are four steps towards honoring our parents:

1. Be honest about who your parents were and are.
2. Take time to both celebrate and grieve your experiences with them.
3. Confess and ask forgiveness for your wrongs against your parents.
4. Make peace, extend mercy, and forgive deeply.

This is not an easy process in most situations, and it may take time and therapy to accomplish this task. However, it is critical to take responsibility for our actions and how we relate to our parents, just as they are responsible for their actions and how they relate to us.

MOTHER

Describe your mother during your childhood years.

What do you remember most about her?

What did she teach you about life?

What would you change about your relationship?

Who is your mother today? What's changed?

If you could ask your mother any question, what would it be and why?

FATHER

Describe your father during your childhood years.

What do you remember most about him?

What did he teach you about life?

Would you change anything about your relationship?

Who is your father today? What's changed?

If you could ask your father any question, what would it be and why?

WOUNDS

CUTS

Children don't get traumatized because they are hurt. They get traumatized because they're alone with the hurt.
—GABOR MATÉ

Our family can be both our greatest benefit and greatest liability. Everyone can expect some level of wounding from even the healthiest family systems. We must learn to acknowledge and accept our story of origin and decide how to move forward with the characters involved.

Did you ever experience abuse or neglect growing up?

Were you ever bullied in school?

What is something you wish you could change about your childhood?

Are there situations or people that you avoid because of past experiences? Why?

HEALING

*"It's not forgetting that heals.
It's remembering."*
—AMY GREENE

All of us have stories we would rather not tell. And yet our experiences, even the ones buried in our subconscious, are deeply formative to who we are.

The initial two steps required for healing are:
1. Properly remembering our wounds and
2. Retelling them to a trusted confidant.

This is vulnerable – it requires a certain level of emotional engagement in the retelling and the witnessing.

Remember: Healing operates on its own timetable. It cannot be rushed and often takes longer than we would like.

What would you like to tell your childhood self? At what age?

Are there any painful parts of your past you wish you could share with someone else?

What stands in the way of sharing hard things about your life with others?

Is reconciliation possible for any of your wounds? What could that look like?

REST & REMEMBER: PERSONAL

REFLECT OVER THE PAST 6 DAYS

"Remember the Sabbath day by keeping it holy."
—THE 4TH COMMANDMENT

BIGGEST ORIGINS CHALLENGES:	SPECIFIC ORIGINS GOALS:
History:	History:
Parents:	Parents:
Wounds:	Wounds:

NOTES:

REST & REMEMBER: PARTNER RECAP

NOTES:

BIGGEST ORIGINS CHALLENGES:	SPECIFIC ORIGINS GOALS:
History:	History:
Parents:	Parents:
Wounds:	Wounds:

RITUAL

ORIGINS

ASSESSMENT

RITUAL

 TRIBE

ASSESSMENT

As adult men, it's important to ask ourselves, "Who am I living for?"

Our tribe consists of the people we live for and those we rely upon.

Tribes include families and friends that share communal values and desired outcomes. The future of any tribe ultimately depends on it's ability to deeply connect on a human level. This is particularly important to note because men often struggle to emotionally connect and be vulnerable.

Embracing our masculinity requires us to model vulnerability and meet the needs of those in our tribe.

FRIENDSHIP

FRAMEWORK

"The only way to have a friend is to be one."
—RALPH WALDO EMERSON

The first relationship we experience outside of family is friendship. Whether through shared interests or social circles, friendships form early and often. As our life unfolds, our friendships broaden. As hardships and crises occur, our friendships deepen. As mutual respect and affection grow, our friendships endure.

How much do you value friendship?

What's required in being a friend to others?

What makes you a good friend?

REFLECTION

"If you have two friends in your lifetime, you're lucky. If you have one good friend, you're more than lucky."
—S.E. HINTON

Our choice of close friends is a clear reflection of our deepest self. They reveal the hidden truths we think about ourselves and the world. Before peer-pressure, there is always peer-preference.

Who are your closest friends and why?

What do they reveal about you?

Are they helpful or harmful in achieving your overall life goals?

Who would you like to develop better friendships with?

How can you strengthen your current friendships?

MARRIAGE

SUITABILITY

"When a wife has a good husband, it is easily seen in her face."
—JOHANN WOLFGANG VON GOETHE

To know if you are suitable for marriage is valuable information when single. It's even more critical when married! If you have been married for a long time, you need to ask yourself again: *"Am I still marriage material?"*

Historically, what type of women have you been drawn to and why?

Do you inspire your girlfriend or spouse to be a better person?

Are you able to financially live on your own? Why or why not?

Do you have any habits or addictions that might negatively affect your relationship?

SEXUALITY

"Having friends with benefits is a lot like communism. It works well in theory, but not so well in execution."
—MILA KUNIS

For men, there are two foundational barriers to living a good life: anger and lust. Distorted views of anger and lust are woven into our sense of what it means to be a man. We must acknowledge that these are particularly relevant when it comes to becoming a good man. We all need deep rooted conviction in how we define sexuality and masculinity.

Who taught you how to love?

Where did you learn about sexuality?

What is the purpose of sex?

Are you comfortable with your sexuality?

In what areas can you grow sexually?

Do answering these questions make you uncomfortable? Why or why not?

PARENTING

PURPOSE

*"Children have never been very good
at listening to their elders,
but they have never failed
to imitate them."*
—JAMES BALDWIN

Our society's relationship with children is extraordinarily complex. On one hand, we are decidedly anti-children. With the advent of birth control, they are viewed by some as an economic liability for both women and men. Almost 40% of children are born to a single parent and many families are isolated without multi-generational involvement in their children's lives.

On the other hand, we also worship children in America. We are spending more time, money, and energy on our children than generations past. The collective consequence of these factors is a loss in the understanding and experience of parenting.

What is the purpose of parenting?

Do you personally want to be a parent? Why or why not?

If you have kids, what do you enjoy most about being a parent?

RESPONSIBILITIES

"It is easier to build strong children than to repair broken men."
—FREDERICK DOUGLASS

A newborn child is highly dependent on their parents for everything for the first decade of their life. And yet, parenting does not come with an owner's manual. Parents are constantly trying to navigate how to best raise their kids in our everchanging world. Ultimately, healthy children have parents who reflect deeply, engage intimately and plan accordingly.

What did you appreciate from your parents' example?

What will you do differently?

List 10 responsibilities of being a parent.

1.
2.
3.
4.
5.
6.
7.
8.
9.
10.

Which of these will you struggle with the most and why?

REST & REMEMBER: PERSONAL

REFLECT OVER THE PAST 6 DAYS

"Most of the things we need to be most fully alive never come in busyness. They grow in rest."
—MARK BUCHANAN

BIGGEST TRIBE CHALLENGES:	SPECIFIC TRIBE GOALS:
Friendship:	Friendship:
Marriage:	Marriage:
Parenting:	Parenting:

NOTES:

REST & REMEMBER: PARTNER RECAP

NOTES:

BIGGEST TRIBE CHALLENGES:	SPECIFIC TRIBE GOALS:
Friendship:	Friendship:
Marriage:	Marriage:
Parenting:	Parenting:

VOCATION

In Latin, the word *vocationem* literally means "a being called." The secret to discovering a meaningful career is to decipher your calling:

Who is calling you to do what?

We all desire to rise to the occasion and answer this sacred call. However, a lot of men feel trapped, uninspired, and detached from their work life. As we rediscover our purpose and align our careers to our calling, the souls of men catch fire and the world changes for the better.

PURPOSE

CALLING

"Outstanding people have one thing in common: An absolute sense of mission."
—ZIG ZIGLAR

Sociologist Max Weber spoke about vocation as an inward calling and possessing a "strange intoxication." Calling is about more than individual passion and self-fulfillment. It is the practical answer to what gives life purpose. The pursuit of our calling illuminates our experiences, cements our identity, and exercises our giftings. Every person has a vocation waiting to be answered.

<u>Skills:</u> What are you good at?

<u>Experience:</u> When has your life felt the most fulfilling?

Contribution: *Who do you want to help, and how?*

Based on the skills, experiences, and contribution you defined, how would you define your calling today?

Refine your calling into one sentence.

Who can you invite into this process?

ROUTINE

*"The quality of our lives often
depends on the quality of our habits."*
—JAMES CLEAR

Each day we are presented with new opportunities to grow into who we wish to become. Change happens from the inside out, so the best routines are formed around your calling. Once we have a better understanding of our purpose, we can order our actions to take small steps towards a more meaningful life.

IDEAL MORNING ROUTINE

TIME	ACTIVITY	REASON
5:00 A.M.		
6:00 A.M.		
7:00 A.M.		
8:00 A.M.		
9:00 A.M.		
10:00 A.M.		
11:00 A.M.		
12:00 P.M.		

IDEAL NIGHT ROUTINE

TIME	ACTIVITY	REASON
5:00 P.M.		
6:00 P.M.		
7:00 P.M.		
8:00 P.M.		
9:00 P.M.		
10:00 P.M.		
11:00 P.M.		
12:00 A.M.		

What are some obstacles to committing to these daily routines?

CAREER

INSPIRATION

"If God gives you something you can do, why in God's name wouldn't you do it?"
—STEPHEN KING

Too often, we settle into careers that provoke an initial sense of satisfaction but, over time, leave us frustrated and aimless. The best careers are anchored in a clear sense of motivation, as it keeps us galvanized to our purpose. Seeking out what stirs our hearts and energizes our souls will help determine a better path forward.

What did you want to be growing up?

How have these aspirations changed over time?

If you were independently wealthy, what career path would you choose today?

Why?

DIRECTION

"Work to become, not to acquire."
—ELBERT HUBBARD

In a world of seemingly infinite possibilities, we are told from a young age that we can be and do anything we want. We tend to adopt a consumerist lifestyle, picking and choosing our friends, spouses, and careers without much thought. Yet, a life not shaped by calling is a life of disorder. Our calling should act as an opportunity guideline for our career.

How does society define a great career?

How do you define a great career?

Where do you hope to be in 10 years?

How do you want your life's work to be remembered?

Are there any opportunities that need to be turned down to focus on your calling?

STEWARDSHIP

MONEY

"No one can serve two masters"
—JESUS OF NAZARETH

As a society, we don't normally talk about personal finances. It's important, however, to acknowledge that a person's true priorities can be found in their schedule and wallet. We live in a natural tension of the "American dream" of maximizing our income vs. pursuing a life well-lived through maximizing our giving.

How much money is enough?

If your house was on fire, which items would you run back in to grab?

In what ways are you currently living beyond your means?

In what ways are you currently investing in your future?

WORK

*"No work is insignificant.
All labor that uplifts humanity has dignity
and importance and should be undertaken
with painstaking excellence."*
—MARTIN LUTHER KING JR.

Our lives, wealth, and relationships are all a matter of stewardship. We have a human responsibility to help creation and others flourish. In short, we are to make things better, not merely accept the status quo.

Have you grown your skills within the scope of your calling?

How have you leveraged your abilities, opportunities, wealth, and relationships in life thus far?

Have you stewarded your life to make the world a better place?

If yes, how so? If no, why not?

RITUAL

 REST & REMEMBER: PERSONAL

REFLECT OVER THE PAST 6 DAYS

"Sabbath is the celebration of life beyond and outside productivity."
—WALTER BRUEGGEMANN

BIGGEST VOCATION CHALLENGES:	SPECIFIC VOCATION GOALS:
Purpose:	Purpose:
Career:	Career:
Stewardship:	Stewardship:
NOTES:	

VOCATION

ASSESSMENT

REST & REMEMBER: PARTNER RECAP

NOTES:

BIGGEST VOCATION CHALLENGES:	SPECIFIC VOCATION GOALS:
Purpose:	Purpose:
Career:	Career:
Stewardship:	Stewardship:

RITUAL

 SOUL

ASSESSMENT

"Spiritual" is something we are and cannot escape. It is our nature and our destiny. There is a spiritual world from which we are designed to draw our life. Therefore, all human flourishing requires a spiritual pilgrimage in which we explore the meaning and purpose of reality itself.

Most traverse these pilgrimages of the soul alone, without a roadmap highlighting their location or direction. However, love and relationships are at the root of reality. The essence of a spiritual pilgrimage is to direct you into a community, into spiritual relationships. There are two types of relationships core to developing deep, spiritual community: *devout guides* and *soul friends*.

LOCATION

POSITION

"We are not human beings having a spiritual experience, but spiritual beings having a human experience."
—PIERRE TEILHARD DE CHARDIN

A pilgrimage is a lifelong journey towards a spiritual destination. We all are travelers on this sacred journey, searching for God and finding meaning and purpose along the way. One way to pinpoint your current whereabouts on your spiritual pilgrimage is by trying to answer some of life's biggest questions.

As best you can, briefly answer:

Where did we come from?

What is the meaning of life?

What happens after death?

Why do we suffer?

How do we find inner peace?

POSTURE

*"There are thoughts which are prayers.
There are moments when,
whatever the posture of the body,
the soul is on its knees."*
—VICTOR HUGO

We as travelers assume many different postures along our spiritual pilgrimage.

- We might **stand** to look forward in anticipation, *or* all around us lost and confused.
- We might **sit** to rest up, *or* to give up.
- We might **lie down** to crawl through tight spaces, *or* to receive help after being wounded

Our journey has led us here and it is not over. To move forward, we must first acknowledge our vantage point.

How would you describe your current posture on your spiritual pilgrimage?

What are the main events that led you to this posture?

What lessons can you take away from this past year?

DIRECTION

DESTINATION

"I try to act as if God exists."
—JORDAN PETERSON

When asked if we believe in God, do our answers put more emphasis on what we cognitively think or on how we live our life? For too long we have framed spirituality merely in terms of cognitive belief: I believe this or that doctrine. It is far better to frame spirituality in terms of your life direction.

FOUR PATHS

As you commit to a spiritual pilgrimage, there are only four directions to explore.

- The *first* path claims there is no spiritual reality larger or other than us.
- The *second* path claims that spiritual truth is primarily found within us.
- The *third* path claims that spiritual truth is primarily found outside of us.
- The *fourth* path claims that spiritual truth is found in a supreme being.

Of these four directions, which paths have you previously traversed?

What discoveries have you made about yourself and reality in the process?

Which of these paths do you currently feel most drawn to? Why?

Have any of these chosen paths helped you become the person you want to be?

Are you currently walking towards an unknown destination, or choosing your own path?

RESOURCES

*"The soul, like the body,
lives by what it feeds on."*
—JOSIAH GILBERT HOLLAND

One of the most profound questions we can ask ourselves is, "What is a life well lived?" Every aspect of our lives is fundamentally framed by our answer to this question. Regardless of our chosen path, we need resources to help replenish and sustain our souls to pursue a life well lived.

What do you currently do to replenish your soul?

Over the course of your life, which resources have benefited your soul the most? Books, music, activities, etc...

Is there a particular resource that you would like to introduce into your life?

COMMUNITY

DEVOUT GUIDES

"Much of what you become in life depends on whom you choose to admire and copy."
—WARREN BUFFETT

Everyone would benefit from interacting with a seasoned explorer on a spiritual pilgrimage. Someone who has gone before, who can identify different hazards, warn against wrong turns, and lead others safely to the end destination. These devout guides have humble hearts, illuminated minds, restored souls, and earnest intentions. They are few and far between. Choose wisely.

Have you ever been mentored about how to pursue a life well lived?

Who are you currently following? Online and in person.

What person or kind of person do you most seek to emulate?

Have you ever asked someone to lead you?

SOUL FRIENDS

"Being surrounded by people on the same journey as you causes you to level up. Your path forward is pretty simple: Decide on your journey and find some people who will cause you to level up."
—SETH GODIN

The spiritual pilgrimage requires time alone, but it is not a solitary endeavor. Due to the relational nature of spirituality and reality, spiritual growth is best achieved by having at least one soul friend. This is someone who acts like an AA sponsor for your soul.

SELF

What do you need in a soul friend?

Do you currently have any soul friends? In your city of residence?

What is the next step?

OTHERS

Which of your friends currently needs a soul friend? List all.

Who do you have the desire and ability to build a deeper friendship with?

How would you invite them into being soul friends?

REST & REMEMBER: PERSONAL

REFLECT OVER THE PAST 6 DAYS

*"We shall not cease from exploration
And the end of all our exploring
Will be to arrive where we started
And know the place for the first time."*
— T. S. ELIOT

BIGGEST SOUL CHALLENGES:	SPECIFIC SOUL GOALS:
Location:	Location:
Direction:	Direction:
Community:	Community:

NOTES:

REST & REMEMBER: PARTNER RECAP

NOTES:

BIGGEST SOUL CHALLENGES:	SPECIFIC SOUL GOALS:
Location:	Location:
Direction:	Direction:
Community:	Community:

NEXT STEPS

*"Any fool can know.
The point is to understand."*

—ALBERT EINSTEIN

PERSONAL REVELATIONS

FINAL IMPRESSIONS:
Health:
Origin:
Tribe:
Vocation:
Soul:

PERSONAL REVELATIONS

FUTURE GOALS:
Health:
Origin:
Tribe:
Vocation:
Soul:

PARTNER REVELATIONS

FINAL IMPRESSIONS:
Health:
Origin:
Tribe:
Vocation:
Soul:

PARTNER REVELATIONS

FUTURE GOALS:
Health:
Origin:
Tribe:
Vocation:
Soul:

NOTES

NOTES

NOTES

NOTES

NOTES

RITUAL

NEXT STEPS

ASSESSMENT

NOTES

"Everyone thinks of changing the world, but no one thinks of changing himself."

– LEO TOLSTOY